THE GOLF
SIMPLIFIED

Compiled & Edited
By
Steven & Lorna Carroll

First Edition

ISBN 978-1-4710-1816-9

PREFACE

Being of the firm opinion that there isn't any need to complicate things more than is necessary, I always smile with gratitude when I come across the word "simplified" as in the context of making any task, be it related to work, a vocation or a hobby, that much easier. And with this simplicity view in mind I have to say that "The Golf Swing Simplified" is an absolute little gem.

The simplification of the golf swing constitutes the chief claim of this little work to a place on the 21st century golfer's bookshelf still. The complexity of the golf swing has arisen largely as the result of the imperfect appreciation of the influence of the wrists in the execution of the movements of the club. Confusion, too, has been introduced by the inaccurate terminology that is usually employed in the description of the "so-called" action of the wrists.

The object of this book is to show that the mechanism of the golf swing depends on "forearm," rather than on "wrist," action. Indeed, apart from putting, it will be contended that there is no such thing as a pure wrist shot in the whole domain of golf.

The exposition, as well as the performance, of the golf swing is a comparatively simple matter, provided the action of the wrist joints can be excluded from the movement. The proof of this proposition is set out in the following pages.

CONTENTS

CHAPTER 1

THE ACTION OF THE WRISTS

AMONG the various implements that have been devised for the propulsion of a ball, there are few which at first sight appear so ill adapted for the purpose as a golf club. Yet the extraordinary accuracy and precision that are exhibited, under the most diverse conditions, by the skillful golfer show that the manipulative difficulties attaching to these clubs are not insurmountable, and it is to the process of acquiring the necessary manual dexterity that golf owes a great deal of its fascination.

There is, of course, no doubt that the best way to learn how to use a golf club is to follow the example and precept of a competent teacher, and to do this as early in life as circumstances will permit. It is hardly possible to learn to play golf from a book, but the written word is not without merit, since the inculcation of correct theoretical principles permits, nay promotes, the making of mental pictures of the perfect golfing swing which may not only help the person who is "off" their game, but also assist the person who wishes to get on to it. Again it is a great advantage to the golfer, especially if they have started to play the game in middle life, to be able to analyze the golfing swing into its component parts, for in this way they are able to discover and correct faults, which from time to time creep into their method of play. Not the least, too, of the pleasures of golf is the working out of manipulative problems in relation to the needs of the individual and the requirements of the game, and in this respect a sound theoretical knowledge of the details of the different strokes is essential.

The great drawback to the written exposition of the golfing swing, as a teaching medium, is the difficulty of describing a series of exceedingly complicated movements in language that admits of but one interpretation. Unfortunately, too, authors of books on golf have commonly paid very little attention to anatomical considerations, and the result has been that their account of the part played by the movement of certain joints in the manipulation of the club has been, to say the least of it, misleading. This criticism applies more especially to the wrist joint, which has had more liberties taken with it, and more nonsense talked about it in golfing circles, than any other joint in the human frame.

It is a very simple matter to demonstrate the movements of which the wrist joint is capable. Let the reader stand with their right hand fully extended in front of their body, the hand in a straight line with the forearm, and the palm of the hand facing the sky. It will then be found that the hand can be bent upwards at the wrist joint (flexion of the wrist joint), or downwards (extension of the wrist joint), or to either side (adduction and abduction of the wrist joint). These four movements, either alone or in combination, are all that can be accomplished by the wrist joint, and it will be observed that, with the possible exception of flexion, they are all comparatively feeble movements from a muscular point of view. Now with the arm and hand in the position mentioned above, it will be found that another movement of the hand can be performed, *i.e.* the palm can be turned over so that it faces the ground (pronation of the hand), and back again to its original position (supination of the hand).

It is the turning over and turning back again of the hand (pronation and supination) which has almost universally been described as a wrist action, whereas in point of fact it is nothing of the sort. The movement in question is effected by the forward and backward rotation of one of the bones of the forearms on the other, and is entirely a forearm action. The wrist joint, so far from coming into play, is passively rotated backwards and forwards *en bloc* with the hand and forearm.

It follows, therefore, that the initial movement of the club head in the backward swing, about which so much has been written, is actuated and controlled by the forearm and not by the wrist, and herein lies the solution of a great deal of the complexity that has been introduced into the golf swing.

The attempt will now be made to describe the swing of both wooden and iron clubs in the light of the conclusions that have just been reached, and it is hoped that the problem of the swing with both kinds of club can, without laboring the point, be considerably simplified.

CHAPTER 2

THE SWING WITH WOODEN CLUBS

THIS little book does not make any claim to be a complete treatise on the whole art of golf; it is put forward rather as a *ballon d'essai* (a tentative experiment) in the direction of illustrating certain aspects of the golf swing.

Thus questions of grip and stance, although of the first importance in relation to the swing of the club, can receive but scanty consideration. As regards grip, there is no question that the overlapping variety gives the most satisfactory results, and it should be employed provided the length and strength of the fingers permit of its adoption, but, if they do not, consolation may be derived from the fact that some of the finest exponents of the game have used the ordinary so-called "two V grip."

The advantage obtained by the overlapping grip is that it makes for the more perfect co-operation of the two hands in the manipulation of the club than in the ordinary grip.

The selection of a suitable stance is a matter of very great importance, inasmuch as the position of the feet in relation to the ball determines to a large extent the character of the swing. At the same time it is not possible to prescribe a stance for any particular player off hand; the question can be settled only by individual experiment and experience. It may perhaps be stated that short, thick-set, muscular persons are better suited by the open than by the square stance, but there are, of course, so many exceptions in this respect that no general rule can be laid down.

Again a feeling of comfort and steadiness on the feet are important factors in the choice of a stance, and the player should take care not to stand with the feet too wide apart. As a general rule the distance between the heels for a person of average height should not exceed sixteen inches, and a much smaller interval frequently adds greatly to the rhythm and power of the swing.

So soon as a satisfactory working stance has been acquired it should, so far as possible, be retained unchanged, since repeated alterations in the position of the feet call for corresponding changes in the swing of the club, and the frequent failure to effect the necessary adjustments is the source of a great deal of inaccurate swinging and timing of the stroke, and generally of much disheartening play.

With regard to the address, there are a few points to which special attention should be directed. The attitude of the player should be so arranged that he feels able to deliver a back-handed swipe at the ball with the left hand. The assumption of this position is facilitated by a slight inclination of the head towards the right shoulder, and by the deposition of rather more weight on the right than on the left foot and heel. Moreover, it is of the utmost importance that the position of the head, as indicated above, should be maintained unchanged until the ball has been removed from the tee. Any shifting of the head into a more upright position in the course of the swing not only alters the level of the shoulders, but also interferes with the balance of the swing, and thereby paves the way to a vast amount of foozling (playing unskillfully; bungling the stroke).

The left hand should grasp the handle of the club very firmly, but not so tightly as to interfere with the flexibility of the muscles of the forearm. The grip of the right hand should be much more delicate, but sufficiently firm to act persuasively.

It will be noted that the position of the two hands on the club is identical in that they are both placed midway between supination and pronation, the natural pose which combines comfort and power.

The player may now address themselves to the business of the swing, and in so doing they should remember to introduce into their methods a little of the *suaviter in modo* as well as the *fortiter in re* (that is, doing what is to be done with unflinching firmness, but in the most inoffensive manner possible).

The preliminary "waggle" calls for no comment

beyond the warning that care must be taken in the execution of this manoeuvre to avoid any flexion of the left wrist. The club head is carried backwards and forwards over the ball by the pronation and supination of the left hand and wrist, the right hand falling in with the movement. The head of the club is now replaced immediately behind the ball, and is slowly and evenly turned away from it by the gradual pronation of the left hand and wrist, supplemented by the rotation forwards of the left shoulder. It cannot be too strongly urged that the whole mechanism of the golfing swing is based on and actuated by these two movements. The pronation of the left hand and wrist turns the club head away from the ball, and the rotation of the left shoulder forward translates the club head upwards and backwards towards the right shoulder. Inasmuch as the left elbow is, or rather should be, kept as straight as possible in the turning backwards of the club, the two movements must commence simultaneously, but the extent to which the one or the other predominates in the initial stages of the swing largely determines the character of the stroke. Thus a rapid pronation of the left hand makes for a comparatively horizontal movement of the club head, whereas a more gradual turnover of the left hand favors an upright swing, and between these extremes there is considerable scope for the gradation of the two factors which control the backward swing. The blending of the two movements must, however, be uniform throughout the backward swing, for experience shows that any deviation in the path of the club head is, as a rule, fraught with disaster. In practice it is found that, as a general rule, the open stance is suited by a more horizontal sweep of the club head than in the case of the square stance, but considerable allowance has to be made in these respects for individual peculiarities. Attention must be directed to one other point, and that is the supreme importance of *commencing* the backward swing slowly and steadily. A very large number of golfing strokes are made or marred in the first few inches of the backward swing, and this observation applies as well to iron as to wooden club play.

The swing may now be resumed, and it will be found that the continuance of the combined movement of pronation of the left hand and rotation of the left shoulder necessitates, at an early stage, the twisting of the body at the hips, and the bending inwards of the left knee in order to permit the shoulder to come round. The proper performance of the body twist, which is the pivot on which the swing turns, is essential to the success of the stroke. The chief, if not the only, danger to the correct execution of the turning movement at the hips is the tendency of the body to sway away to the right, which not only throws too much weight on the right leg, but completely disorganizes the swing of the club. The commission of this almost irremediable golfing *faux pas* (false step) is prevented by a very simple device, which consists in resisting the turning forward of the left shoulder by a stiffening of the muscles of the right leg. This manoeuvre not only prevents any swaying of the body to the right, but keeps a proper share of the weight on the fore and inner side of the left foot, which, in consequence of the bending of the left knee, and the raising of the heel from the ground, should press firmly on the turf and maintain the balance.

The continuation and completion of the backward swing now resolves itself into the full development of the two factors which initiated the movement; that is to say, the club head is turned inwards (*i.e.* as regards the body), backwards, and upwards to the top of the swing by the twisting of the left forearm and upper arm (pronation of the left wrist and hand), and of the body (rotation of the left shoulder forwards). It is by means of the combined twisting of the arm and body that the sensation of tension is acquired at the top of the swing to which attention has been directed by Braid (James Braid – champion golfer 1870-1950) and others.

At the top of the swing the grasp of the second, third, and forth fingers of the left hand should be relaxed just sufficiently (but no more than this) to allow the shaft of the club to drop behind the head into a horizontal position, with the toe of the club pointing towards the turf. The wrists at the top of the swing should be situated immediately beneath the handle of the club, and it will be found that the left wrist and hand are fully pronated and the left wrist joint slightly abducted (a pure wrist movement, which not only facilitates the falling back of the club behind the head, but also its recovery at the beginning of the downward swing).

The position of the right hand and wrist at the top of the swing is the same as it was in the address, viz. midway between pronation and supination. The right elbow should not be kept glued to the side, but should not be separated from it by more than a few inches. The upward and downward swing of the club are part of one and the same cyclic movement: there should be no interval between them, and they should be attuned into a rhythmic whole. The commencement of the downward swing waits pendulum-like on the completion of the upward and backward motion of the club head, and should take up, and fall in with the time and pace of the movement.

As in the case of the upward swing, it is the beginning of the downward movement which largely determines the success or failure of the stroke.

There is a tendency, due to the throwing forward of the hands and arms at the beginning of the downward movement, for the club head to take the shortest route from the top of the swing to the ball, a proceeding which is productive of a great deal of inaccurate play, since it not only lets the right shoulder into the stroke too quickly, but allows insufficient time for the hands and arms to act effectively. The whole stroke is rushed through too rapidly, and anything like accurate timing of the ball is rendered impossible.

The object of the player should be to make the path of the club head between the top of the swing and the ball as long as possible, and this is attained, not by throwing out the hands and arms to the front, but by letting them go backwards and to the right at the commencement of the downward swing. Vardon (Harry Vardon champion golfer 1870-1937) especially insists on the importance of getting the club head behind and to the right of the player at the beginning of the downward swing, and there can be no doubt that this manoeuvre is of the greatest assistance in the timing of the ball, and in bringing about accurate and powerful play.

The commencement of the downward swing, then, finds the head of the club taken backwards and to the right by the gradual tightening up of the fingers of the left hand on the handle of the driver, by the straightening of the left wrist, and by the turning back of the left hand into the halfway position between pronation and supination. The club, by these means alone, is brought two-thirds of the way down towards the ball, and from this point onwards the whole spring and force of the untwisting and rebound of the upward movement, in respect both of arms and body, are brought to bear on the acceleration of the club head which is lashed through the ball.

The pace and power of the club head at the moment of impact are greatly increased by the incipient pronation of the right hand, which contributes the whip-like snap to the movement whereon depends so largely the length and straightness of the drive. This scarcely perceptible turning of the right hand is due to the tightening up of the grip at the moment the ball is struck, and is almost universally ascribed to so-called wrist action, whereas of course it is nothing of the kind. On the contrary, it is a pure forearm action, which takes command of the wrist and hand together, and although at the moment of impact the movement is largely potential, it develops into full pronation of the right wrist and hand *en bloc* ere the finish of the stroke is reached. It is, moreover, a very powerful movement, and one of which the wrist joint is totally incapable. The player must, however, be cautioned against a too early accentuation of the turning over of the right hand, in view of the danger of foundering the ball, or of producing a disastrous pull.

After the ball has been dispatched from the tee the club head must continue in the line of flight unchecked to the full stretch of the arms, and should then be brought round over the left shoulder with the hands in a position the reverse of that at the top of the swing.

The body also comes round in consequence of the rotation of the shoulders on the pivot of the hips, so that at the finish of the stroke the chest of the player faces the line of flight of the ball.

The bending inward of the right knee and the transference of the weight from the right to the left foot, which accompany the turn of the body, should assist in the completion of the follow through, and it is well that some weight should still be left on the fore and inner side of the right foot at the finish of the stroke.

The tendency of the body to sway forwards at the moment of impact should be resisted by immobility of the head both as regards position and pose, and by retention of the weight on the right foot and leg until the ball has been dispatched from the tee.

There is very little more to be said about the mechanism of the golf swing in respect to wooden clubs, except by way of insistence on certain essential features of the movement.

It should be borne in mind that the hands describe in miniature the path of the club head, so that any disturbance in the lesser swing of the hands is enormously exaggerated in the greater swing of the club head. From this point of view, therefore, it must be strongly urged that the combined turning movement of the hands and shoulders in the upward swing should be free, smooth, compact, and uniform, and the player must take care to swing well within themselves in order to cultivate the feeling of complete control of the club head at all stages of the stroke.

The club head, too, should always move in advance of the hands as well as of head and shoulders, for it is essential that it should be in possession of the lead from the beginning to the end of the swing. The player is strongly advised to stereotype their stance, as there is nothing more prejudicial to accurate swinging and timing of the stroke than repeated changes in the position of the feet. Great importance attaches to correct foot action, and to this end the weight should be kept well back on the heels. The bending inwards of the left knee, and the raising of the left heel from the ground, should not come too hurriedly into play during the early part of the upward swing; a little restraint in these respects exercises a remarkable steadying influence on the turning movement of the arms and body. The necessity for keeping the eyes on the back of the ball has not been mentioned for the reason that this precaution will always be observed, provided the position and pose of the head be maintained unchanged throughout the swing, until the ball has been struck from the tee.

The importance of the forearm movement in the execution of the golf swing has already been insisted upon, and if the arguments that have been advanced carry weight there is no necessity to pursue the subject further. Attention may, however, be directed once more to the danger of stiffening up the muscles of the forearm in the address, or during any portion of the swing. Even at the moment of impact, when some tightening up of the grip of the right hand is inevitable, the muscles of the forearm should be kept perfectly flexible and free from any trace of rigidity.

Finally, the player should bear in mind that the golfing swing is essentially a combination of "pull" and "push," in other words "a pushed pull," the left hand, arm, and shoulder actuating the pull, which dominates the stroke, the right hand, arm, and shoulder controlling the push.

CHAPTER 3

THE PLAY WITH IRON CLUBS

THERE is practically no difference in the principles which govern the play of iron as compared with wooden clubs. The instructions, therefore, which have been given with reference to the swing with wooden clubs apply with equal force to the stroke as played with iron clubs. The alterations in stance and swing that are necessitated by the use of the shorter iron clubs call, however, for certain modifications and adjustments in method of manipulation which require examination and explanation.

The fact, also, that the stroke with iron clubs is to all intents and purposes a distinct hit introduces a factor which is dormant in the swing with wooden clubs.

The circumstances which demand the use of the iron require that the handle of the club shall be gripped very firmly by both hands, since any wobbling of the head of the club as the ball is struck is fatal to the success of the stroke. At the same time the muscles of the forearm should not lose their flexibility, but the whole stroke must be played with a firm, crisp, and forceful compactness.

The stance is narrower with iron than with wooden clubs, and the less the distance the ball has to travel the more restricted becomes the stance in order that the necessary turn of the body can be obtained without disturbing the immobility of the feet.

The shorter shaft of the iron club not only obliges the player to stand nearer the ball, but also necessitates a more upright swing than in the case of the wooden club.

The upward movement of the club is actuated and controlled by the gradual turning over (pronation) of the left hand in conjunction with the rotation forwards of the left shoulder. The latter movement together with the bending inwards of the left knee and the raising of the left heel from the ground should be much more restricted and restrained than in the case of the swing with wooden clubs, and on no account should the left heel be allowed to turn outwards.

Steadiness on the feet and a compact swing are the foundation of success in play with iron clubs.

The upward movement should be performed very deliberately, with the left elbow as straight as possible, and the greatest care must be taken to prevent any swaying of the body to the right, or any changed in the position and pose of the head.

There is no advantage to be gained by taking a full swing with iron clubs; a three-quarter shot, besides giving much better control, obtains practically all the length that can be got out of the club. With this proviso, the distance required is regulated by the length of the backward swing, and it is customary to speak of quarter, half, and three-quarter iron club shots.

Whatever kind of iron club shot is played, the head of the club is brought into contact with the ball from the top of the swing with a sharp, crisp, and determined flick of the forearms and hands. In the case of the ordinary stroke the club head is forced through the ball and the turf immediately beneath it by the right hand, which takes command of all shots played by iron clubs. At the finish of the stroke the shaft of the iron should be found in the line of the flight of the ball and more or less parallel to the ground, with the right arm fully extended and the face of the club looking towards the left of the line of flight.

Immobility of the head is even of greater importance in iron than in wooden club play, and any swaying or lifting of the body in the upward and downward swing is destructive both to accuracy and length. In all iron shots it is absolutely essential that the club head should take the lead in the upward swing and retain it throughout the stroke.

The manipulation of the club with the right hand and forearm is the key to the playing of iron shots of all kinds, whether with the #1 iron, #5 iron, or #9 iron. It will not be possible to do more than outline the general principles which regulate the various kinds of iron shots, but their practical application should not present any real difficulty to the player who is prepared to devote the necessary time to the practice of the different strokes.

In the ordinary iron shot described above, the flick of the club head as it is brought into contact with the ball, which is so essential to the success of the stroke, is obtained by the potential turning over (pronation) of the right hand. At the moment of impact the sudden tightening up of the muscles of the forearm brings the right hand and forearm from the position of slight supination to the position midway between pronation and supination; and this movement, in conjunction with the straightening out and extension of the right elbow, imparts the characteristic flick to the club head.

The further the club is carried beyond the horizontal position at the finish of the stroke (and though this extension of the swing is unnecessary, it is frequently observed), the more pronounced becomes the pronation of the right hand and forearm. A very slight exaggeration of the movement of the right hand at the moment of impact gives rise to a pulled ball, which is not uncommonly a source of trouble in iron club play. A firm grip with the left hand and the exercise of a little restraint in the turning over of the right hand is usually sufficient to cure the tendency to pull with iron clubs.

The spin that is imparted by the pronation of the right hand causes the ball to travel a considerable distance after it pitches, and for this reason the manoeuvre in question is most clearly in evidence in the playing of the so-called "running-up" shot (running-up shot, an intentionally low shot designed to roll on to the green, which is usually played with a lower lofted iron such as a #6 iron or lower). For this stroke the ball, which should be in a line with the right foot, is hit cleanly and accurately by a shorter and somewhat more rigid movement of the club head than in the case of the ordinary iron shot. Immediately after impact the pronation of the right hand comes into play and steadily turns over the club head, which is carried forwards low down and parallel with the ground to a finish which should not take the shaft of the club much above the horizontal position. The "running-up" shot can be played by any iron club, which gives the stroke a very wide range of application.

The right hand instead of being turned over (pronated) may be rotated in the opposite direction (supinated) at the moment of impact, so that both the palm of the hand and the face of the club are looking upwards at the finish of the stroke.

This type of shot is employed when a high ball with little run is required, and although it may be executed by any iron club, it is usually played by a #5 iron or #9 iron. In all shots that entail the raising of the ball into the air, it is well to bear in mind the necessity of keeping the weight well back on the right leg until the ball has been struck.

The push shot (a shot played severely to the right), at once the most difficult and important of all iron strokes, differs from the ordinary shot in stance, swing, and finish. Of these by far the most momentous is the finish, as will presently appear.

For the push shot the player should stand rather nearer to the ball than usual, with the weight inclined forwards on to the left foot, and the hands slightly in front of the ball. The upward movement is controlled almost entirely by the arms, which take the club slowly, smoothly, and somewhat stiffly out and away from the body (*i.e.* in front of it) to the top of the swing. The action of the body is restrained by keeping the left heel in contact with the ground during the upward swing. The face of the club is brought directly down on to the REAR-MOST PORTION OF THE BALL from the top of the swing, and at the moment of impact the club head is pushed through the ball by the *vis a tergo* (i.e. the force from behind) that is produced by the simultaneous stiffening of the forearms, extension of the elbow joints, and slight forward movement of the body. After impact the rapid relaxation of the muscles of the forearms permits of a follow through, which is not so pronounced as in the case of the ordinary iron shot.

CHAPTER 4

ON PUTTING

NO manipulative difficulties arise in connection with the ordinary straight-forward use of the putter. The putt is, or should be, a pure and simple wrist stroke. Moreover, it is the only stroke in the game of golf that is played solely by the wrists. The chief, if not the only difficulty in putting consists in the elimination of all extraneous movement. A correct wrist action is very easily acquired, and when it is combined with confidence in the calculation of the effect of local conditions on the run of the ball, the player is equipped with everything that is really necessary on the putting green. There are very few, if any, putts that cannot be negotiated in this simple way, but, inasmuch as the line to the hole can frequently be made less tortuous and difficult by virtue of the addition of spin or side, as the case may be, to the ball, the means by which these refinements are introduced into the stroke must also be briefly considered.

So long as the stance does not interfere with the action of the wrists it does not appear to matter very much how the player arranges themselves on the putting green, but an easy and natural position promotes consistency in the accurate hitting and control of the ball. A firm, flexible grip of the putter ministers to the delicacy of touch which is so essential to the persuasive propulsion of the ball along the path to the hole. The attention should be concentrated on hitting the ball accurately and firmly, and the intrusion of the least movement of the head, legs, or body must so far as possible be prevented. The face of the putter should be placed immediately behind the ball, at right angles to the line of the putt, and the club head is then swung slowly and steadily straight backwards along the turf by the flexion of the left wrist, the right hand and wrist falling in with the movement. The length of the backward swing is regulated by the length of the putt.

The forward movement of the putter is controlled almost entirely by the right hand, which by flexion of the wrist joint brings the head of the club smoothly, firmly, and somewhat crisply into contact with the back of the ball, and then carries it through to a finish along the line of the putt. The action of the wrists must not be checked at the moment of impact, or at any other stage of the swing, for the least semblance of a jerk is fatal to true putting.

Care should be taken not to move the head or look up until after the ball has been struck, and the player should also remember to putt for the back of the hole.

When the question arises of counteracting the influence of slopes or undulations on the green, or of alterations in surface conditions, or of wind, etc., the putting problem from a purely manipulative point of view becomes a much more complicated matter.

The running power of the ball can be increased or diminished, or its course can be diverted, by the introduction of spin. Forward spin or "run" is communicated to the ball by hitting it below its center with a rising club head, while backward spin or drag is obtained by striking the ball above its center with a falling club head.

In order to procure forward spin in practice the player must stand with the wrists slightly behind the ball, which should be rather nearer the left foot than usual, so that at the moment of impact the club head has passed the lowest point of its swing and is rising to the finish of the stroke.

Conversely, backward spin or "drag" is obtained by having the ball nearer the right foot, and by bringing the club head on to the ball before the lowest part of the downward swing has been reached.

It is possible to graduate the amount of spin that is imparted to the ball. Thus the amount of forward spin can be emphasized by increasing the steepness of the upward swing of the club at the time, and immediately after, the ball is struck. Again, drag can be augmented by a downward and forward push of the club at the moment of contact with the ball.

Generally speaking, "run" is required for uphill putts, and drag for downhill putts, but practice alone can provide the experience necessary to decide the kind and amount of spin that is required in particular circumstances.

Lateral spin or side is obtained by bringing the head of the club across the back of the ball at the moment of impact. The course of the ball can be deflected to the right, or left, according as "cut" or the opposite spin is communicated to the ball. "Cut" is obtained very readily by drawing the head of the club inwards across the ball at the time of impact. Deflection of the course of the ball to the left is a very difficult and hazardous undertaking, but it can be accomplished by passing the club head across the back of the ball from within outwards. The ball should be addressed by the toe of the club, and at the moment of impact the club head is taken across the back of the ball from within outwards by the straightening out (extension) of the right elbow joint, the right wrist remaining in the position midway between supination and pronation. "Cut" is used in order to make the ball run round a stymie (an object that is in the way of a golfer's shot and lies between the golfer's ball and the green, i.e. a tree), and also to counteract the influence of the slopes on the green. For instance, a slope running from right to left (in respect of the line to the hole) causes the ball to run to the left, so that if it is struck with "cut" which deflects its course to the right, the opposing forces tend to neutralize each other, and the ball can therefore be played in a much more direct line to the hole than if it had been played without "cut".

The attempt to deflect the course of the ball to the left is very rarely advisable, but it is sometimes impossible to negotiate a stymie by any other means. Side spin should be used only when circumstances imperatively call for its employment. The habit of playing all strokes on the putting green with more or less "cut," that is favored by some players, interferes with the true hitting of the ball, which after all is the most reliable means of getting the ball into the hole.

CHAPTER 5

COMMON FAULTS
HOW TO AVOID AND HOW TO CORRECT
THEM

IN this chapter the practical application of the general principles underlying the golfing swing that have been advanced in the foregoing pages will be considered in the light of those deviations from the strict path of rectitude which commonly beset the average golfer in their course round the links. Faults of omission as well as of commission will come under review, and these will serve as a text for the purpose of illustrating the distressing effects of any serious departure from correct methods of swinging. In this way, by a careful survey of their golfing indiscretions and delinquencies, the player is frequently enabled not only to locate the source of their trouble but also to apply the appropriate remedy. A correct grip of the club combined with a suitable stance are factors of the first importance in the building up of a steady, reliable, and consistent swing. The essential feature of the grip is that it should be made with the fingers and not with the palm of the hand. A finger grip promotes flexibility of the muscles of the forearm, increases the feeling of "touch" of the club, and in this way encourages leverage and adds to the speed of the club head. A palm grip, on the other hand, stiffens the muscles of the forearm, stiffens the swing, diminishes power, and leads to a heavy, clumsy style of play which possesses neither length nor direction. The fingers of the left hand should hold the shaft of the club firmly, even tightly, and this steady grip should be maintained throughout the swing. The grip with the fingers of the right hand, at all events during the address, should be so regulated that it is distinctly subservient to that of the left. The two hands are brought as closely together as possible, and in such a way that the knuckles of the left hand are facing the line of flight of the ball, while those of the right hand look in the opposite direction. In a word, the grip of the club must be characterized by firmness with flexibility.

The stance adopted by the player exercises a most potent influence on their swing; for, as is so well expressed by Taylor (J. H. Taylor champion golfer 1871-1963), the golfer must either adjust their swing to their stance or stand according to their swing. Inasmuch as it is easier to alter the stance than the swing, it behoves the player at as early a stage in their golfing career as possible to find a find a suitable stance—that is, a stance which fits in and harmonizes with their swing. Repeated changes of stance entail repeated changes of swing, and it is remarkable, even in the case of an experienced player, how small an alteration in the matter of stance will completely disorganize the swing and lead to the most disastrous results.

The adjustment and maintenance of a suitable stance are not such an easy matter as is commonly supposed. There are days when everything goes well—when, without mental or bodily effort, the ball is driven from the tee with the most satisfactory results both as regards length and direction. On these occasions it not infrequently happens that with increasing confidence a gradual but imperceptible alteration is introduced into the stance and the drive is suddenly lost. It is well therefore, with an experience of this kind, to carefully examine the stance before proceeding to the adoption of more drastic remedial measures.

The question of how to obtain a suitable stance still remains to be considered, and although the groundwork of the performance, so to speak, can be outlined, it is by practice, and by practice alone, that the solution of the problem is ultimately achieved.

The selection of the open or square stance, or some combination of these two positions, appears to be a matter of indifference, and so long as the swing harmonizes with the stance that is adopted, it may be left to individual choice and experience. In addressing the ball the player should stand firmly on their feet, with their toes slightly turned out and with the weight thrown well back on the heels, the right heel taking rather more of the weight than the left. The distance the player stands from the ball exercises a profound influence on their swing, but it is impossible to lay down any hard and fast rule on this matter. If, however, the upper parts of both arms are in contact with the sides, as they ought to be, the distance the player should stand from the ball very largely adjusts itself. The elbow and knee joints should be just sufficiently relaxed to do away with any feeling of stiffness, and the poise of the body generally should be as easy and natural as possible. A slight inclination of the head to the right conduces not only to the proper disposition of the weight, but also enables the player to obtain a better view of the ball, which will shortly claim a larger share of their attention.

It will appear therefore that from a golfing point of view there is a wide range of choice in manoeuvring for position on the tee, and so long as the manner of standing combines, within the prescribed limits, a feeling of comfort and power the question of a suitable stance may be regarded as settled.

The preliminary "waggle", which should neither be too extensive nor too prolonged, enables the player to test their golfing machinery both as regards their position in relation to the ball and the "feel" of the club, and also as regards the flexibility and harmonious working of the muscles concerned in the initiation and control of the backward and forward movement of the swing.

The mechanism and forces concerned in the actuation and performance of the golfing swing have already been fully considered in Chapter 2, and it is necessary here to refer only to the causes which lead to the imperfect performance of this procedure.

The turning over of the left hand which initiates and controls the backward movement of the club head should be performed smoothly and moderately slowly, and in no circumstances should any suspicion of a jerk be introduced into the movement. The player should have complete control of the club head throughout the entire swing, and although swinging slowly they should feel able to swing at a still slower rate should the occasion arise for so doing. The pace of the forward movement must always exceed the pace of the backward movement, and herein lies the necessity for the complete control of the backward swing. It is essential, too, for the proper performance of the series of events comprising the golfing swing that the player should cultivate a sense of rhythm, for it is the appreciation of the time relation between the backward and forward movement that enables him to bring about that gradual acceleration of the pace of the club head which reaches its fullest development at the moment of meeting the ball.

A very large proportion of the ills that golfers are

heir to originate in faulty body movement, and although the co-operation of a properly executed corporeal twist (body twist) is absolutely necessary for the successful performance of the golfing swing, it must always be subservient to the action of the hands and arms.

The chief difficulty arises in connection with the turning of the body at the hips. Instead of turning at the hips, the player sways their body, and with it their head, away to the right—a proceeding which completely disorganizes their swing and, except in the case of an expert, leads to irreparable disaster. The fact is that the body should never take an "active" part in the performance of the golfing swing, but should remain a passive instrument under the control of the hands and arms. It is also important to bear in mind that the poise as well as the position of the head should remain unaltered until the ball has been dispatched from the tee. A correct turn of the body at the hips is controlled and regulated by the action of the feet and legs, which, under the stimulus of the swing, maintain the equilibrium while the trunk and shoulders rotate. A firm position of the right foot and leg resists the tendency of the body to sway laterally, and assists very materially in keeping the position and level of the head unaltered. A gradual and uniform inward bend of the left knee during the backward swing, combined with a steady pressure of the fore and inner part of the foot on the turf, makes for level swinging and a correct turn of the body at the hips; and see to it that the left heel in rising from the ground does not shift from the position immediately over the one it occupied during the address.

Summarized briefly, the backward swing is initiated and controlled by the left hand and forearm, which, with the help afforded by the rotation forwards of the left shoulder, twists and translates the club head backwards and upwards until the shaft reaches a horizontal position over the right shoulder. At the top of the swing the wrists, which are both abducted, should be situated immediately beneath the handle of the club. The abduction of the wrists (a pure wrist movement) is an important feature of the position at the top of the swing, inasmuch as it allows the shaft of the club to assume a horizontal position without any loss of control. It also facilitates the recovery of the club at the commencement of the downward swing, as will presently appear. Furthermore, the abduction of the wrists does away with the necessity for any loosening of the grip of the club at the top of the swing, which has been advocated and taught by some authorities on the game.

The various other details connected with the position at the top of the swing are already familiar to the player and hardly require any further consideration.

The initial movement of the downward swing largely determines the success or failure of the drive. There is a tendency, more especially when the back-ward swing is unsteady or has been imperfectly controlled, for the player to throw out their hands and arms at the commencement of the downward movement, and in this event the club head takes, so to speak, a short cut down to the ball, with the most disastrous results so far as the accuracy and rhythm of the swing are concerned. The path of the club head between the top of the swing and the ball should be made as long as possible, and to produce this effect the hands and arms, and with them the club head, must be thrown, not forwards, but backwards and to the right, by virtue of the straightening of the abducted wrists at the beginning of the downward swing. The wrist action at this point is almost precisely similar to the movement of the wrists that obtains in the throwing of a fly, and when properly executed it is of the very greatest assistance in the timing and control of the downward swing.

The completion of the downward swing is, as already explained (see pgs. 20-21), a comparatively simple matter so long as the club head has been directed into the right path at the beginning of the movement. The player must, however, remember to keep the club head not only in front of the hands but also of the head and shoulders, and it is meet that they should show some reluctance in transferring the weight from the right to the left leg in the completion of the follow through. At the finish of the stroke the body should be facing the line of flight of the ball, with the hands well up above the level of the left shoulder and with the poise of the head and body unaltered in their relation to the ground. The weight at the moment of impact, but not before, should be transferred from the right to the left foot, and at the finish of the swing should be mainly on the left leg and foot, though the fore and inner part of the right foot should still bear a part of it.

Before leaving the subject of the drive with wooden clubs, the player may be again reminded that a very large percentage of errors arise in connection with unsteadiness of the head and body. The head may move upwards or downwards, as well as from side to side, and any of these irrelevant actions are fatal to the success of the drive. Pulling and slicing, topping and schlaffing, are among the numerous ills for which these aberrations of cephalic (head) and corporeal (body) pose are largely responsible. If, therefore, evidence of one or other of these deviations from the clean and true hitting of the ball make their appearance it behoves the player to institute a careful investigation of their swing, more particularly with regard to leg and body work.

Two other faults call for passing mention, the more important of which is over-swinging. The over-rotation of the left shoulder (in which, of course, the right shares) not only introduces a feeling of restraint and interferes with a comfortable and enjoyable view of the ball, but also tends to make the player lose control of the club head, and as a consequence the clean hitting of the ball and the timing of the shot are prejudicially affected.

The other departure from correct methods is found in the improper use of the right hand and arm, more especially at two points in the swing. The right hand, beyond steadying the club, should not interfere in any way with the backward movement of the club, which must be controlled entirely by the left hand and forearm.

Again, in the downward swing at the moment of impact it is of great importance to avoid a too rapid turning over of the right hand on account of the danger of foundering the ball or of producing a most egregious (extremely and noticeably bad) pull. The introduction of the influence of the right hand in the forward swing should be restrained until the straightening of the wrists at the beginning of the downward movement is completed. From this point onwards the right hand and forearm are largely in control of the swing, but their influence should be exerted steadily and uniformly.

The chief causes of faulty driving may be briefly summarized as follows:

(1) Alterations of stance without corresponding adjustments of the swing.

(2) Failure to keep the weight well back on the heels, and more especially on the right heel, during the address and throughout the swing.

(3) Defective back swing. The left hand and forearm may fail to control the backward movement of the club, which is consequently rushed or jerked up to the top of the swing by the action of the right hand and arm.

(4) Imperfect body action. Instead of turning at the hips, the body, and with it the head, may sway away to the right in consequence of faulty footwork, and more particularly of the turning outwards of the left heel during the upward swing. The same result may also be produced by the mistaken introduction of power supplied by the body muscles. Swaying in the downward swing may be due to active interference on the part of the body muscles, or to failure to keep the weight sufficiently long on the right leg during the forward sweep of the club head. The moving of the head at any period of the swing until the ball has been dispatched from the tee is probably productive of more trouble to the golfer than any other fault they can commit.

(5) Failure to let the club head take the lead throughout the swing. This usually means either failure to initiate the upward and backward

movement of the club head by the turning over of the left hand, or to failure in throwing the club head backwards and to the right by the straightening of the abducted wrists at the commencement of the downward swing. From the start to the finish of the swing it is essential that the club head is in front, not only of the hands but also of the head and shoulders.

(6) Inability to swing and hit as hard as possible without pressing.

So long as the swing is in order and the power is supplied from the proper sources it is unnecessary to restrain its display. Pressing does not mean the application of too much force, but its introduction from an improper source.

With regard to the play with iron clubs it may be remarked that the faults committed by the player are for the most part very similar to those they display in the use of the #1 wood or #2 wood, and usually as the result of like causes. The distinctive features of iron as compared with wooden club play are a nearer approach to the ball in the address with a narrower and less mobile stance, a firmer grip more especially with the right hand, a more restrained and altogether more compact backward movement of the club, and the introduction of a distinct hit into the forward swing. The mistakes that are made with iron clubs arise most commonly in connection with the stance and swing. The average player is apt to stand much too far away from the ball, and in addressing the object of their attentions fails to place the sole of their club from heel to toe in contact with the ground, and at right angles with the line of flight. Over-swinging and failure to maintain complete control of the club in the backward swing are frequent sources of trouble, and a want of crispness and decision in the hitting of the ball is a common cause of inability to obtain the full effect of an iron shot.

Since the distance required in the case of iron shots is regulated by the length of the backward swing, the supreme importance of obtaining complete control of this movement does not call for any further demonstration. Furthermore, the straightening of the wrists at the commencement of the downward swing for the purpose of directing the club head backwards and to the right, to which attention was called in the case of the drive, applies with equal if not greater force to the playing of iron shots.

In respect to putting, the worst fault the player can possess is want of confidence. Among lesser evils are unsteadiness of the head or body, and defective wrist action. Attacks of what may be called "green sickness" are most commonly due to one or other of these causes. The putter must be controlled by the wrists, and by the wrists only; then, provided the head and body are kept perfectly still and the ball is hit firmly and confidently, with a good follow through of the club head along the line to the hole, there is very little more that can be done to ensure the success of the stroke.

CHAPTER 6

A LITTLE THEORY AND SOME PRACTICAL HINTS

THE view put forward in this book that the golfing swing is initiated, controlled, and operated throughout by the forearms has met with very wide acceptance, but the exclusion, to a very large extent, of the influence of wrist action (as such) has been the subject of some adverse criticism. The objections that have been raised to the exclusion of wrist action are more apparent than real, and turn, for the most part, on the question of the extent to which the action of the wrists assists in the manipulation and pace of the club head.

It will be admitted at once that wrist action is in evidence, to a varying extent, in almost every type of golf shot, but it has been and will be contended that this factor is merely accessory and altogether subsidiary to the main business of the swing. A brief analysis of the swing will serve to illustrate the argument by which the soundness of this proposition is established.

The turning over (pronation) of the left hand is, of course, the initial movement of the backward swing, and this manoeuvre is carried on to, and completed at the top of the swing. The right hand falls in with the swing of the club, and this necessitates the immediate extension of the right wrist, and with it some supination of the hand at the beginning of the backward movement (a most important feature of the swing). The continuation of the swing in conjunction with the bending of the right elbow culminates in the turning over (pronation) of the right hand, so that at the top of the swing both hands are fully pronated. In point of fact, therefore, the top of the swing finds both hands fully pronated, but in reverse directions, and both wrists more of less abducted.

In the downward swing the movements of the hands and arms that have just been described are, to all intents and purposes, reversed so that at the finish of the swing both hands are again fully pronated and again in opposite directions.

In other words, the golfing swing is dominated by the turning of the hands, through the action of the forearms, from pronation at the top of the swing to pronation at the finish of the swing; a manoeuvre which generates both pace and power. In this movement there is no room for wrist action except in so far as it contributes to the smooth and sweet running of the golfing mechanism, and enables the forearms to keep the club head in front of the hands and shoulders.

Wrist action comes into play at the beginning of

the swing with the extension of the right wrist; at the top of the swing with the abduction of the wrists and their subsequent adduction; and finally at the moment of impact, when the left wrist is extended. All these movements are accessory and accommodative, and in no circumstances can it be shown that wrist action adds either substantially or directly to the power or pace of the club head.

This brief summary of the theoretical position of forearm action in relation to the golfing swing is capable of considerable extension, but the exposition that has been given must suffice to answer the various objections that have been urged against its paramount importance in the manipulation of the club as compared with wrist work.

The practical application of some of the theoretical considerations that have been advanced require examination, and this will be done as briefly and succinctly as possible.

Inasmuch as the display of forearm action depends on hand and finger work, the question of the most suitable method of gripping the club immediately assumes considerable importance. It is essential that the club should be gripped by the fingers, and more particularly by the forefinger and thumb of each hand, and less tightly by the second, third, and fourth fingers. Get the shaft of the club into the crook of the forefingers of both hands, and keep it there by the pressure of the thumbs, is the advice given by the majority of professional players, and it is no doubt sound, for the reason that it promotes the flexibility of the forearms. Any stiffening of the forearms is fatal to the success of the swing, hence the importance of gripping the club lightly by the second, third, and fourth fingers.

The backward swing of the club should be loosely, easily, and smoothly performed, and care should be taken to avoid any suggestion of rigidity or stiffness, either in the arms or shoulders, or for that matter in any other part of the golfing mechanism. The extension of the right wrist and the bending of the right elbow should be adjusted to the turning over (pronation) of the left hand. In other words let the left hand turn lightly, smoothly, and freely over the right hand to the top of the swing. It is at this phase of the swing that trouble most commonly arises. There is a tendency to rush the initial period of the downward swing; to let the hands and shoulders get in front of the club head; and when this happens nothing in the nature of a golfing swing can possibly materialize. It is vital to the success of the swing that the club head should be kept in front of the hands and shoulders throughout the whole swing, and the golfing mechanism is full of subtle devices to secure this end. At the beginning of the downward swing time must be found for the adduction of the wrists, which throw the club head in front of the arms, hands, and shoulders. The hands and arms then carry on the movement to the point of impact with the ball when the extension of the left wrist in conjunction with the turning of the right hand from slight supination (*vide supra*) to incipient pronation maintains the lead of the club head, and gives the whip-like snap to the movement which is so essential to straight and powerful driving.

In the performance of the downward swing from the start to the finish of the movement, it is of the utmost importance that the various parts of the golfing mechanism, and especially the wrists, arms, and shoulders, should be kept as loose and flexible as possible, since any tendency to stiffness (except in special circumstances) is prejudicial to the making of the stroke.

It seems hardly necessary to observe that the remarks that have just been made apply (*mutatis mutandis* – with the necessary changes having been made) with equal force to the play with iron clubs.

One other point calls for remark, and is that the player should not, of course, think of their forearms, or indeed of any other part if their anatomy when playing a shot. Inasmuch as the forearms operate through the hands and fingers only, it is merely necessary for the player to concentrate on so manipulating the club head that it is kept in front of the hands and shoulders, and thrust through the ball.

So long as the club head is kept in front

of the swing, and the rest of the golfing mechanism is working freely and flexibly, without any suspicion of stiffness, the success of any stroke should be assured.

THE END